Weather watch!

Published by Evans Brothers Limited
2a Portman Mansions
Chiltern Street
London W1U 6NR

Reprinted 2007

Consultant: Dr Naima Browne
Publisher: Su Swallow
Design: Neil Sayer
Editorial: Debbie Fox
Picture research: Julia Bird
Production: Jenny Mulvanny

British Library Cataloguing in Publication Data
Lawson, Julia
  Weather watch!
  1.Weather - Pictorial works - Juvenile literature
  I.Title
  551.6
  ISBN 978 0 237 52921 5

First published in paperback in 2005

Acknowledgements

The author and publisher would like to thank the following for their kind help:
Richard Johnson and all the staff at Southfield Primary School, London W4, the parents of the children photographed and the children (in page order from the title page): Michelle James, Eva Elks-Hermannsen, Raman Oraha, Christopher Kwok and Aaron James.
The Early Learning Centre for the use of a range of their toys.

Printed in Dubai by Oriental Press

How to use this book

- Always remember that reading together should be fun!
- Reading with young children involves more than simply reading the words on the page. Talking about the pictures and ideas and linking them with children's experiences provide invaluable learning opportunities.
- Most children will enjoy an adult reading the book to them for the first time. Some children will want an adult to continue doing this, whilst others may prefer to have a go at reading the book themselves.
- Don't worry if children don't read the words that are written on the page. Young children often make up their own text! As the book becomes more familiar, children may remember the text and 'read' it back. This is an important stage in learning to read, so encourage children by being an appreciative audience!
- The book introduces new ideas and vocabulary. Don't expect children to take in everything at once. You will need to linger over the pages children find particularly interesting.
- Children learn by asking questions, so try not to rush through the book and be prepared to answer children's questions.

Activity boxes
- This book includes some ideas for activities that will deepen children's understanding of the concepts introduced. The activities range from simple rhymes to practical investigations.

Notes and suggested activities
- On pages 20/21 there is a useful reference list of storybooks, videos and CD-Roms, as well as further activity suggestions.

Weather watch!

Julia Lawson

Photographs by
Peter Millard

Evans Brothers Limited

We are very hot! We are staying in the shade.

Phew! It's too warm. We're cooling down in the paddling pool.

Brrrr! We feel chilly. Jumping up and down may help us to keep warm.

We are feeling warm and cosy. We're wrapped up snugly.

Dragon Smoke
Breathe and blow
white clouds
        with every puff.
It's cold today,
        cold enough
to see your breath.
Huff!
    Breathe dragon smoke
        today!

Lilian Moore

It's been raining. We're going to leap and splash in the puddles.

No rain today! So I'll need to water the plants.

Make a rain gauge

This rain gauge is very easy to make. Take a plastic lemonade bottle, cut it in half and make a simple scale along the side with sticky labels. Put your gauge outside and after it has rained, go out and measure how much rain has fallen.

She is soaking wet and needs to dry her fur.

They are hot and dusty. They need a wash!

If it rains too much, there can be a flood, but ...

... not enough rain makes the ground dry and cracked.

Have you ever heard the weather?

crunchy snow ...

Howling wind ...

booming thunder ...

dripping rain.

Can you see the colours of the weather? Big black clouds, silvery rain, white lightning flashes.

Bright blue skies, fluffy white clouds, dark shadows.

Can you make a weather picture? What colours would you use to show it's warm and sunny? What colours would suggest it's cold and wintery? What about cloud and rain?

Sometimes we see all sorts of weather, even on the same day!

Fog, sunshine, snow, wind. What's your favourite?

Notes and suggested activities for parents and teachers

We hope that you have enjoyed sharing this book and have tried out some of the additional ideas found in the activity boxes. Feel free to adapt them as you wish. For example, another nice way of exploring the idea of weather colours is to make a rainbow using children's handprints. Listed here are some children's storybooks, videos and CD-Roms that link to the theme of weather, along with suggestions for further activities, songs and games. Have fun!

Build your own Weather Station

As well as the rain gauge (page 9) you can also make a wind sock to show the strength of the wind. Take the inner tube from a roll of kitchen towel and decorate it. To one end, attach a small piece of wood such as garden cane. To the other, attach some streamers made from strips of tissue paper or ribbon. The wind socks can be 'planted' outside and they will look lovely fluttering in the wind. Another way children can herald the wind is to make some wind chimes. Simply hang some objects such as shells, buttons or beads onto some string and attach the string to a small hoop.

Weather Games

Fan Race Place some ping-pong balls in a line. Each player uses a paper fan to move his or her ball to the finishing line. Children can also play this game using straws.

Musical Weather This is a variation of musical chairs. Place lots of pictures of different types of weather, for example the sun, raindrops or clouds. When the music stops, call out a type of weather, such as thunder, fog or frost and the children have to run to the appropriate picture.

Match the Weather Give the children some weather-related clothes and objects, such as a raincoat, a sun hat or an umbrella. They also need a set of weather words and pictures, for example sunny or thunder. The children have to match the right weather word or picture to the appropriate object.

Songs
What's the Weather? (to the tune of 'Clementine')

What's the weather? What's the weather?
What's the weather like today?
Is it snowing? Is it icy?
Is there fog or is there hail?
Is it raining? Is it windy?
Is it cold or is it hot?
Are there clouds or is there sun?
Is the weather nice or not?

I hear Thunder (to the tune of Frere Jacques)
I hear thunder, I hear thunder,
Oh don't you? Oh don't you?
Pitter patter raindrops,
Pitter patter raindrops,
I'm wet through, so are you!

I see sunshine, I see sunshine,
Oh don't you? Oh don't you?
Fluffy clouds in blue skies,
Fluffy clouds in blue skies,
I'm warm through, so are you!

Storybooks
Kipper's Book of Weather, Mick Inkpen, Hodder
Out and About, Shirley Hughes, Walker Books
Elmer's Weather, David McKee, Andersen Press
Alfie Weather, Shirley Hughes, Bodley Head

The Wind Blew, Pat Hutchins, Red Fox
Bringing the Rain to Kappiti Plain, Verna Aardeema, Macmillan
Noah Built an Ark One Day, Colin & Jacqui Hawkins, Mammoth

Videos
Kipper *The Big Freeze and Other Stories*, Hodder, Hit Entertainment plc
Kipper *The Snowy Day and Other Stories*, Hodder, Hit Entertainment plc
Percy the Park Keeper *After the Storm*, Hit Entertainment plc
Little Bear Lost and Other Stories (includes 'The Rainy Day'), Carlton Entertainment
Old Bear and Other Stories (includes 'Jolly Snow'), Carlton Entertainment
Winnie the Pooh *The Many Adventures Of Winnie the Pooh* (includes 'The Blustery Day'), Walt Disney Home Videos

CD-Roms
Pingu and Friends, BBC Multimedia
Smudge the Scientist, Storm Educational Software
The Magic School Bus *Kicks Up a Storm*, Scholastic

Index

animals 10, 11

blue skies 17

chilly 6
clouds 7, 16, 17
cold 7, 17
colours 16, 17
cooling down 5
cosy 7

dry 13
drying 10
dusty 11

flood 12
fog 19

hot 4, 11

keeping warm 6

lightning 16

paddling pool 5
plants 9
puddles 8

rain 8, 12, 13, 15, 16, 17

shade 4
shadows 17
snow 14, 19
sounds 14, 15
sunshine 19

thunder 15

warm 5, 7, 17
wind 14, 19

Photography acknowledgements
page 10: Natural History Photographic Library © Yves Lanceau
page 11, 12, 13, 16, 17 (left): Still Pictures
page 17: Robert Harding Picture Library © Lee Frost